ALL THE PRETTY LIGHTS

Gerry McGrath has published two critically-acclaimed collections, *A to B* in 2008, and *Rooster*, which was shortlisted for Scottish Poetry Book of the Year in 2013. He received a Scottish Arts Council New Writers' Bursary in 2007 and a Robert Louis Stevenson Fellowship Award in 2004. His pamphlet *Love All The People* (2021) confirmed his place as "one of the most acute and moving observers of our lives". His poems "alter the reader and benefit our humanity".

PRAISE for *All the Pretty Lights*

The secret wish of all lyric poetry is to stop time, Charles Simic tells us, and Gerry McGrath understands this viscerally. He brings those blessed tools - craft, image and line break - to build rafts on which to sail the river Lethe. These poems speak to our senses, probe deeper; they make a lasting impression.

— Ilya Kaminsky

Gerry McGrath is a master of a kind of unsettling lyricism that compels attention. When he beams the reader up from a stanza you never really know where you are going to rematerialise. Spare, mellow, brittle, vivid by turns, this is a poetry whose statements and conjurings respect the surrounding silence.

— David Kinloch

McGrath's book takes a completely different direction from pretty much the range of current Anglophone poetry, refreshingly so. Steeped in – and unafraid of – continental European culture, the poems here create dreamscapes and dream logic, claiming and re-activating a hitherto underused Surrealist inheritance. They play tricks with and on the reader, dance delightful speech-steps which are in turn dainty (those meditative stanzas of pivoting short lines and their pauses) and complex (those macro-structures which bring the almost-random into the ordering sense of an anarchic catalogue). Though the poems appear at first delicate, at times tender certainly, there is a boldness here. As one poem tells us: 'Poetry is a summons / to courage'. Before such an invitation, we can only dive in and swim within these remarkable texts, invigorated.

— Richard Price

ISBN: 978-1-916938-32-8

Cover designed by Aaron Kent

Edited and Typeset by Aaron Kent

Broken Sleep Books Ltd
PO BOX 102
Llandysul
SA44 9BG

CONTENTS

if time is a homeland

grey chicken legs of the box hedge

now memory smiles at memory

fat kings slumbering in wild garlic

owned a blind telescope, slipped into mythology

binds the sisterhood of colour & form

a day that looks & smells like roast chicken

for Kate, Liam & Owen

All the Pretty Lights

Gerry McGrath

Broken Sleep Books

if time is a homeland

BELVEDERE

So they were sitting beside the belvedere, in shade.
And they were drinking, barely exchanging a word.
The sun was shining and words were beyond them.

Past the low stone wall lay the river. Further off,
lost in the thin blue air, were the island's three peaks
yet to exist, as if they existed.

A breeze got up; the world tilted and water, seen
slopping up the side of a glass, pushed the air ahead,
carrying birds, the clink of ice, notes of lemon.

On the lawn children ran like small dogs, yelping
with a mix of terror and joy, and occasionally
a mother or father appeared to gather them in.

He thought there must have been days
when people forgot even that they had gone to sleep
and woken, re-born.

That they had flowed, like the river behind
the wall flowed, huge and still and countless,
grey as all rivers are grey.

The sun continued to shine and the breeze blew fresher
and he drank again and thought
in the eyes of small dogs days like this will come again.

BY PORTENCROSS

1

It doesn't matter autumn writes in
the blue sky in the empty blue sky
the wrangled leaves shorn blackthorn
lie   It's me

talking to you in the only way I can
Under the coming rain tenderly
A song lost a long road walked asleep
The way half moss
                        half burnished stone
It doesn't matter the silver secrets
we live to keep

2

Light & shade we walk together
fingering the old bones the bracken
for syllables   you point
at the ghost of a barley field & beyond
The sea's own music topped with sheep
eyeing us like caught thieves Scattered

in their own time a line of purple turnips
like a headhunter's grizzled trophies jangle
& plead Lord how to raid the darkness
for the sustenance we need

3

Was it the early seasonal gift
of oystercatchers on the Montfode
that had me running for first base
For the uncertain embrace
                              of a bomb shelter
Not the universals please God
Anything but the universals

4

I wait for you in my human soup
of pea-skins & anarchy

Alas castle you're on sabbatical
in silence

Where do you dream you are
untenanted shells at your feet

They were wrong   Whoever said
we two should meet

5

You come comely
Through the golden wrappers
of childhood

Like twigs of spring
Unlikely   a peewit

at a live angle
to the full-grown night

Love passes
From ventricle to ventricle
Out of sight

STENDHAL IN TRIESTE

Et puis je vous oublie
Le plus fort que je peux

My Dears
I wonder if you are listening
in your dancing palaces
Behind the window wire
What indeed you make of it

                           all

Forgive me if I sound despondent
The mid-afternoon sun is slanting in

I've no doubt the animal gesture is real
However I must tell you how often
he rejects the facts

Poor fruit he calls them   scales that fall
From the passing comet of a moth

FOR EXAMPLE TRAMPOLINES

Rocking faintly on the Earth boat it stops
Long enough for me to check my pulse
To see how I am before I leap
In that high way

Is the lesson human dignity
Or a cry for love   clickety
Click I hear the dockyard from everything
To a pause
O sweet mother of affection the neighbours
Are knocking through a wall
Heaven forfend the imaginal clock screams wide
                              its punishing hands

I ASK

Island, what would outdo you for blueness, I ask.
River runs, the bonny zigzags. Thumbnail Alps, I ask.

A non-native of water I am fished to a gin-clear
syllabary by speckled others. Word-blind, I ask.

Street gangs worry at a sense, ah the shambling pine.
Houseflies in radical departure board choppers. Tickets, I ask.

Summer bends, Autumn returns to you, unbidden.
The window panes gleam, dark fangs half-smiling, I ask.

Stone lyre, you are too close for me to dream you.
Who would carve his name in a country without words, I ask.

The heart is also mute, the visible electric steam.
Limited to its own form, a valve opens, a valve shuts. I ask.

A sorry regime's ear catches the shredding of wills.
Love's ablaze, is this a house that cannot shake the fire, I ask.

The exigent Spanish poet wrote verse sweetened
By tender advice bright with lemons; what sense is this, I ask.

Staccato raindrops head south. Gravity or
The call of the great silver factory. A cup of water, I ask.

Paris or Bologna, the scholastic's wintry dilemma.
Needlework or a quiet night sitting in front of the telly, I ask.

Bach's nocturnal crepitations, a pluvial sarabande.
O Universe, why do we wait for night for you to fix, I ask.

If time is a homeland, remember me before I existed.
Island, let me rival you for love, age happy, with no sad drumbeat, I ask.

grey chicken legs of the box hedge

FLEAS

after Gottfried Benn

His neighbour returned early

For months next door had resembled
The inner workings of a slipper factory

Now the silence was broken by nocturnal
Footsteps on the hardwood floor

An elective conversationalist she seemed
Distracted *Irreplaceable documents*

The scene that greeted him later at home

- grey chicken legs of the box hedge
- the fist of a metal spade
- spam (about fleas) from the vet

SNOW BUDDHA

Time never lay so heavy
As the snow that made
              you

White-mouthed
Letter-boxed
              mouthed
Addressee
Of our old
              selfhoods

So what's the story
Are we really
              cool witnesses
To our own vibrations

Is that it

How wonderful
& sad

Half of me was expecting
              more

HISTORY LESSON 1979

He said

:

You know

there are two Europes

The one we know

about wealth

& control

And the other

about slavery

& desire

Every morning

birdsong denies them

both

HOLY INNOCENTS

for Aidan Paisley

is that
        starlight
or streetlamp
        lint
on the put-upon-window

everything need not
        be
disowned sadness

AFTER THE GAME: **18 (36) HEMISTICHES**

They turned a blind eye
                    poured rosé on the petunias

Four feet of foxglove leaning
                    up periscope!

Attendance was otiose
                    he horsed the edible flowers

Like soft fruit
                    mislaid in marble

One immigrant foot
                    a life of hyphens & vowels

New wine new bottles
                    clarty glasses

You are absolved of all sins
                    vobiscum in futuro

City gates fastened
                    the sentries chewing hay

Bringing down the rowan
                    ladder rope saw

Water music

        Handel's oarsman's night sweats

Her sting remains intact

        an apiarist's grief

Cavafy's at the door

        oh wait a minute

The Spanish handmaidens

        ugly as sin

Lucien's still life

        quail feathers in the spittoon

Late summer winds

        an army under the turning wheat

Your sons & daughters

        ancient as you were

Unconditionally

        a modern European democracy

Poetry & the internal market

        a business case for the soul

now memory smiles at memory

OCEAN OF LONGING

I'm pretty sure this is all
because you exist   It's only
I want to burn the hillside entire
Every tidy heathered knap
                              buckshee sap
I'd gladly pour down the neck
of that silly man of yours

But then the least balding of
the tea-time chimpanzees
a propos of Harpo's outsize hat'n coat
                              indifferently
slopes for a pint   In me kindling
an epipelagic light of dawn
crests the brae of those big goodbye
                              gangster shoulders

OTHER WOMEN

Sunk in the mainstream
          of the world's water
I tend to the audibly
          inaudible sounds
Of dried & polished cutlery
          slippered in the silver silt
Of a sea-going drawer

          next to mine
Her lovely wrists   o how
They explained things   eyes pealing
A softer pebbly light

They would have us unhappy women

Now memory smiles at memory
Of these & other ignorances
          I was guilty
Over the sweetest of puddings

POSTWAR

Like a safe cracking
the rain clicks
          unpicks
the road for home

Hidden Sought
the underground crew
wakes to sleep
one-two one two
Flying

from a somewhere
dream to close
the claws of a ship's bell
breaking through

[RED]

Red holds light
Cloud above the thumbnail
Peaks   O so

                  prophetic
                  prophyletic

Doyou write poetry yourself
Sitting at your cool-cat table

Lick your lips for the pink
Undersilk

Sweet meats
Of the mildly talking rooks

Is your hot head from the tiger's flame

How I envy you
The half-light

                  half-life

What was that again about
The island

Send me a postcard from
                  your edge
Sir please do

LOVE IS

Here's another for your lovely cloud You
up there caring for your distracted father
Mother by Glasgow's shipping flanks I care
for you a lot do even love what a fine word
Love is what can match it I wish I could say

But the great dragons of fire are calling
The words are as ever chaperoned waiting
for us waiting for something more secret
more intimate more telling than ourselves

fat kings slumbering in wild garlic

OF SMALLER GARDEN FURNITURE

Reason shakes
him from the partisan
clutches of sleep
His expression hangs
a question mark
over the rickety staircase
of unread books
He scratches his chin
balancing on one leg

At times
he looks like
an early Christian saint
a martyr
whose faith is a test
of the world

At others
he is soulful companion
freely giving up
the long white tooth
of solitude

The face far-fetched with fear
rage disappointment ecstasy
is moved by minor displays
                            of tenderness
Goldfinches at the feeder

The fresh scent of cherry blossom
Fat kings slumbering in wild garlic
A first love that died of old age
The unfulfilled promise of smaller
garden furniture

HANG BLUE ORANGES

How like us

Tiptoeing among the green
Tea lights

To turn ashen
When that feline mouth
Its lifted corners
Smiling so

In a grievous age
Hang blue oranges

GUILLÉN'S AIR

Geordie your poetry's a reminder
We give our song to men
Who sell the moon
       *

What peoples the see-through
Soil stands with its eye
To a tympanum hillside

Bellying out the old yarn
Poetry's rich in princes
                  & damask

How quiet through the air goes
That other air unversed

Danced to the tune
Of a slatted balcony
Yellowing heady bare

SUPERLUNARY

To write
Nothing for the Institute
of Nothing

Poetry is a summons
to courage

Confident as a clock
Spring gives the word

to fly through the great halls
pressed in your fancy

Test the limbs of those
proud sweet wild colours

      prouder

          sweeter

              wilder

than ever

soft midwinter of my rainbow colours

TAPTOE

Past the town's startled edge
the maps the books Past
the army of sallow faces
in the shadow of ancient litter

the old gossips
whisper up their sleeves
like courtroom lawyers

A rat blearily
from a siding pauses sniffs the air
left & right asks

What time is this
What century is this

On the platform's tablecloth
trains come & go blue uninterested
Dragons fold their wings are still
The boulevard is elsewhere

Children cry at a cafe table busy
as the losing corner
Bluebottles with kingly pride
rise & fall rise & fall drowsy
on forgotten meridians

A mother an aunt weeps
Biting the dry wine stain on
your top lip you pray not knowing
the words for her forgiveness

UP LAW HILL

Not now who knows when
We'll crunch the same white
Numbers the same prepositions
Up Law Hill behind us
The mast ahead the field
Dumb with sheep one hundred
Two hundred slow
Like fairground horses o

My love I am not here
I am there in the soft lanterns soft
                    midwinter
Of my rainbow colours

Have you heard

Snow posts words
In the commentator's coat hanger
                    mouth
Clouds rise out of the saddle
The camera believes in us
It's why we run

TEA

Feels
the childhood of memory

Listens
while a braid of water
flows from the equine shiver
of the spout

ENGLISH HARMONICS

Shaggy big-boned
conifer
all fingers & toes

you need me so
that I might see you
autumning in

the hairdresser's brisk
nor
noreasterly

Elsewhere
in a time of hats
              & innocence
a chameleon

waiting for
the music of the distances
to converge

sits
tongue's length
from a grub

that moves with the speed of the faithful
through the tea lights
of a green-shuttered room.

YOU'LL NEVER MEET THE BOSS

Law is
Pleasure is law

A voice without authority
Claims

An elephant is standing
On the crocodile in the room

A mountain's weight
Feels in its shadow

Law is
Pleasure is law

in Asia's lowland forests a house of grief

WAVES

A stiff neck above the art
Trapped in my frame
I dream of childhoods
A buoy hauling the glue
Bones of a horse
Across skittering pier sides
You

Puffing your last puffaw
The roped hands easy
                              in earth in water
Rocking the ship's bear-toy
                              on your knee

Like the tide
By the rocks of Malta
                              a wave
To learn not all of nothing
Of nothing at all

CASTLES

i.m. Patricia McGrath Ellis

They appeared looming unlit
Towers each an echo of the other
Dark-flecked toothsome equal

Parts of your ship-sized self
Dreamy with star struck
                    lore
Fending Moorish slavers
From the shore

What happened happened

Thunder fell mute
The rain stopped listening
Nowhere stood
                    in Asia's lowland forests
A house of grief

A late piratical sweep found
Reason's end   unbound
So were we
                    knee-deep
In East Bay sand
                    a needful disarray
                    the separating voices
At play

ISLAND MOON

You know how much I love
to watch you suck in those
hollow cheeks mouthing the words
oh I don't think so I really don't
think so

In our blue garden the company
is mixed a blush of pears & ruined
cherry leaves I am looking up out
at a gull on the roof tucking its wings
into a brown paper bag

If it pleases you please
let it not be a hair shirt a resident heron
or the same old very old fires   but

the hours the air
a mayfly dance that lie
deeply
sweetly in the arms
of the summer play
I feel so close

warming me
even now

I'M OVER HERE

Late October   in
the kitchen of your beautiful home
drinking tea from a *queen-of-fucking-
everything* cup

We get round to knowing
loneliness is also olfactory

Spark's cruellest writing
says what's sayable
What does your nose tell you about me

Let me speak as a Russian nurse
Let me whisper   the real stories
are never told

rivers swim uphill

CHINESE WHISPERS, A DOWN-TO-THE-SEA SCAPE

Sunburst
   sun dust
     blink of a hill

pear trees
   bare trees
     absolutely still

car horn
   blackthorn
     washing on the line

yellow gorse
   meadow horse
     a midge's serpentine

Tree stumps
   neat clumps
     of *pis-en-lit* and grass

cracked walls
   jackdaws
     bouncing on the paths

flat roads
   flat toads
     never made it over

park bench
   chaffinch
     wagtail and plover

Lay lines
   parking fine
     the Princes Serendip

celandine

        scots pine

                wild strawberries in a strip

warning signs

        brambles spines

                Golfers shouting FOUR

caddies

        Irrawaddies

                a wee burn tickling oer

Shetland ponies

        with their cronies

                small waves in a dwam

bladderwrack

        seaweed-black

                babies in a pram

mountain top

        glottal stop

                collies off the leash

man o wars

        round ae applause

                fae two crows on the beach

Sonsie tugs

        sleekit subs

                inching down the Clyde

water mark

        basking shark

                where does all this hide

dolphins

        endorphins

                set loose by the sight

of sand eels
      grey seals
            stretching in delight
Innocuous
      binoculars
            venture down the Isle
contours
      meridian
            town & country mile
jamjars
      beetling cars
            oysters in the bay
hay bales
      monkfish tails
            belties munching hay
Rhyming slang
      the old gang
            onomatopoeia
power station
      weird notation
            coal ships at New Year
horseback
      natterjack
            riders riding pillion
rock pool
      nursery school
            shore crabs dance cotillion
Mute swans
      fruit scones
            a buried arquebus

rook squadrons

        traffic wardens

                unum e pluribus

hedgehogs

        equinox

                wintertime departs

reveille

        diwali

                light around the heart

LOST ALBUM TRACKS OF THE 70S

How good to hear from you Its
been a while Does the trailing sax
of unsilence still get on your nerves
Wasn't it a form of loathing Don't be
afraid remember you are also here
to be entertained   There will always be
enthusiasts for spinning humming
crackling in the undergrowth of sound

Yes I walk the backbeat county ways Still
receive the cold kiss of the abstract

                                    implement
ghosting on the coastal path unsexed
by the civic placement of metal benches
that fairly freeze the bum O for
a soft-mouthed dog to flush the bird
Root-a-toot brother galoot whose shoes
his deeds never quite matched I'm happy
You're welcome any time with eyes blind
I'll keep looking over my shoulder   Guess
against the cool pane whose lips   Hissing
furrow of youth that stopped being

                                    your place
& mine

ELECTRIC BRAE

O Sirs little knights
you are on a bus
to Culzean

where if you're lucky
they'll let you slip your knots
sit up unwellied on your knees

stare at the castle
                    as it is
listening for the sea

They being your teachers
eyeing a lonely vertical
scribble on their cuffs
a stargazer's plan B

now the clouds have bubbled
& the last of the dragons
                    is gone

FOUND PICTURE

O and it makes the bones so sore to feel how embarrassed I was at the very thought of disowning all the downtrodden days that lay me next to you. The slick perfume of your gaze & the spring tide stealing us both from the toes up. How embarrassed, indeed. I knew one man capable of it, divine he was. & those that came after, flat pebbles thrown by curious hominids that bounced off the big megaliths, they were men too. Men & women who dipped their pens in the great dragons of light. I admired them as well. But here I'm with you on this coastal plain, perpendicular. My big box head's been centuries lost in the garb of the benevolent masters, all the good lines are breakable, my implement's unsteady & anyway the wordless edges of this wave and that are busy eddying at my feet.

HIPPOCAMPUS

Between the meagre, chalky stream,
the full-on flood, I can't say how long
I've lived. You happened along, hips
swaying, my first American. Tall,
coffee-skinned, hair like late-afternoon
sun slanting in a small upstate town.
Did we get on? We drove over lemons.
A river swam uphill. For a while after
you'd gone I walked among the pink
marbled columns, twisting, winding
blood of slaves. I still have memory.
My hand cupping your breast, yours
mine. I think it's true. Rivers swim uphill.
I hear words, then water. What else
might I expect? On and on. Overnight
rain spirals from its source.

are you seen by the roses in bloom?

POMPEII

In a life without walls its the pause
Stops the train in its tracks the look
Caught looking over the shoulder
At the last facts of other people

Has an old friend blown in from the war
Time is on a horse fading   the way
To the next village next hour next
Heart beat disappears fast

The stage designers in knee-high
Killer disguise   step

ash blind into the ransom
                              shadows

EVERYONE IS

You are there, my shape,
my table-daughter, my thorn.
The old conjuror had it wrong.
Something familiar if not memory
lingers in the polished wood.
Who dares ask: are you seen
by the roses in bloom?
Do they peer into your pain
like editors to the edited?
Twist their mouths in hollows
while you become landscape, tree,
a pick to chip at the prize ground
now everyone is dead & gone?

THE OLDER QUEEN VISITS ENT

Rain then wind
like curative hands
islanding pain

More magical she
shoos away
monstrous limbs

In her lipstick thirties
felt
in a saltier thrapple

the red gills
suddenly

PENELOPE RUNNING

Penny. May I call you Penny? Perhaps
You'd be happier with the pigeons
Under the eaves where not even Laertes
Would think to look for you.

While you faithfully unravel
Someone than me less leadered
Will perform the utterly thinkable   so
When dear Odysseus returns & the blinkers

                                                    are off
I'll miss you

                                                Penelope running
Between home & the dark songs   that pitilessly
Carry you away.

owned a blind telescope, slipped into mythology

THE PEOPLE ON THE LAWN

The People On The Lawn
Were invisible were not
On first-name terms with the dead

Waved maniacally at passing cars
Said their goodbyes by postal ballot

Nodded at the thinning poet
Made their own darkness

Were uninterested in the light from Liébana
Fished in their youth

Won countless Petrarchan laurels
Woke themselves from pisspoor dreams

Suffered from chronic distraction
Never knew what they'd missed

Owned a blind telescope
Slipped into mythology

Were doomed to love's sequel
Called the Fire Brigade

Admired the body's embroidery
Were as pale as hosts

Held one end of the silver braid
Thumped their hearts in prayer

Earned long-service medals
Broke wind inside the city walls

Wore rust petals in their hair
Struck coins

Launched a mouse hunt
Tied all their loose ends with logic

Were exposed from mid-thigh to shin
Understood betrayal as
                              a slow circulation in the veins

ENDLESSLY

Endlessly you write
The square mile down

A lost embrace
        my wondering

What waters make
The stones bloom
The furious blades
        of summer

Break the soil
for syllables

I'D BETTER GET UP

for Katherine Kilalea

The secret's out
morning's a bone
the unflanneled face
of a curling stone

Am I allowed to say a robin
before the invention
                              of sound
burning with the news
in a Southern hemisphere
they found the divine particle

in the shape of a woman's hand
waving goodbye waving
goodnight

o my arbours my uncompetitive
linocuts
be good enough to tell me

in the slack-jawed betting yards
who now cares who calls
black from white

AMONG NEVADANS: 26 FIRST LINES, HEADLINES, FISHING LINES

You can only be too clever once

Leave them wanting less

You'll know what time it is by the playground chants

If that doesn't work, ask the dug

A poem deserves to exist

While tap-dancing on the mantelpiece

To be filed under interesting local
                    flora & fauna

Then [he] Stendhal counted her freckles

Beekeepers of Nevada support
                    natural human fragrance

Nationalism for beginners – a syllabus

Damaged goods? You should see the van

The only human awake lives in this house

Extinguish

A pause – let the blackbird swallow its spittle

Oddly enough, a career in marketing

Alder, meet rowan

Sunkissed, eyes closed, water warming
                    to cream

That sound – sawing wood or furiously
                    testing a zip

Miracle worker shown leniency

Cloud coming in on the tide

Rook at the funeral checking its wings

Gooseberry netting – a poor-looking tent!

Hedda takes a stand
                    at the school Summer fair

An incredibly soft 'c'

Po-faced conger orders the langoustine

Pigeon sniggers past, its tail sweeps the stage
                    clean

SO UNIFORMED THE QUIET VICTIMS OF DESPAIR

On reflection
It could've been anywhere

A great balance surrounds
The docile verities of sisterhood
Both stand because we fall

By increments
Milk comes to the boil
Pressing on labile matter
Testing eternity

Their splendour

binds the sisterhood of colour & form

THE MAKINGS OF A GOOD CONVERSATION

If the dead could speak, who wouldn't
give himself to honeyed afternoons
in their company, to the cool judgement
of the mind meeting the everyday?
The male sits in a languid seat.
In the street opposite a tree unknots
a crooked branch to a nib, sketches
a pianist's long-fingered promenade,
the mineral indecency of light.
It's a lie the seasons click their heels.

In the rearview, a tick-tock heart
clocks the captain's perfumed daughters
finalising their hair in the honest glass
of urban children. They wonder, sometimes
aloud, sometimes not, how long
in the surrendering heat of an August evening
their dark fruit can endure.

A SMALL PIECE OF THEATRE

Before I entered
something about how sunlight
traps the shadows
led me to believe I'd find
in your outstretched limbs
dreams reaching with ease
with awe across the tributaries
of rucked cotton

an inlet
of respondent rhyme

There is always an immense sadness
that pads gently
across the prism of the body

Calls home
where the furthest sound
takes flight

On your chest I often think
the white speckle
                extends

along a migrant paw
to know the scratching post
a labyrinth
night

In some minute explosion
begins to love quivering in its acts
your gathered form   light

FOND & ANCIENT HISTORY

I prefer to believe
Lightning begins
On the ribbon's edge
We call horizon

Sparks & dies
        in a breath

Binds the sisterhood
Of colour & form
        momentarily

If we accept mystery
As the moment when

BIRDS

A French salad with mouthfuls of goat's cheese
so small they gave you cutlery from a doll's house
& hoped you wouldn't notice You said nothing
How many of these have there been how many
places mouths how many dinners cups of nut brown
coffee From another table the jangle of horse
brass Hussars in the pay of the king not paying the
slightest heed to the caged whose folded wings
sap the strength of blood & men Up there Up there
Hurrah & metal flashing The low wallpaper dimly
admiring your insouciance Shadow of a crane
enshrines the feeding arm Answer me this you say
parrying the green stemmed pause between second
hand & endive What you don't say is what you do
How are we to be How are we to live when they come
knocking at our door Silently we settle our feathers
Peasant chairs surround a table scattered with bread
rind the ultimate crumbs of a superior circumstance

GOYESCA

after Mina Loy

1.

Flung to the moon
Straw *Pelele*
Watches the night
Shadows bloom
                    shrink

Majas in their livery
Under drawn

Behold
The bird-economies
Plumed in syllables

The lunar dust
Of Goya's jig

Rise from a body
In trampoline rags
                    outsize wig

2.

Life-substitute

'Tween dance

         & word

He peaks

In the higher air

Face haunted by the sun

A kinder science rolls

Across that lenient tongue

Blasé, glassy-eyed

To the marbled prospects

That once were he

         Paree

         to the cooked meats

         of Bowery

Preferring languor

Sky-worn bliss

To the idling coma

Of a sculpted wrist

3.

Gravity brings him
                    down
Unmarked from jinks
With the cracked
                    larks

To the calf-skin bed
Of the tauromachs

Feeling atoms of disgust
The time-served *majas*
                    weep
Rouge their cheeks
Draw the blanket
                    let him sleep

GERMAN LOWLAND FORESTS

What did we imagine, at such a price,
in the void offered us; that this is how
the spirit leaves the body, pale shoulders
rising from the ageing coolness of a sheet,
the slow migration of rain. The hilltop
is clear. Unlovely the finger of partition
that curled inside you. Loneliness needs
poetry to exist. Up there, in the stillness
disarmed by birdsong, how helpless how
mildly we receive the boars of oppression.

a day that looks & smells like roast chicken

FRANCIS CADELL ON IONA

Something exploded generously
on East Bay
                something happened
to change the paint   there are all
but the innermost sounds
                                & signs
The rocks wordless beasts
bury in a powdered canvas
their heads come over all hushed

A bright-eyed field paints me real
From this field nods green the scene
already in my eye of a picture ending
before it begins in the time
                                before time

A cool feline asks: is there laughter
in what you say to your hiding gods

You take in the kelp the bladderwrack
Salt grass erupts in the breaking garden

AND ALSO THE SON

I know you're there
when you've gone

It's like falling in love
in some eatery

You order everything
the laughter echoes

I'm looking through
yellow paper
at a day that looks
& smells
like roast chicken

Nowhere should be
this shadow-free

I'll know you're there
when you've gone

I THINK PERHAPS

Apple blossom
like a small white bell
grows slowly

Has no memory
of what it's going to touch

I think perhaps
I should find eternity
in a puddle
by the school gates

Come at it
like a hunchback
with a knife

MY BROTHER LIVED LIGHT-HEARTEDLY

He was on the road at twelve
Came back ten years later
Out of a sense of duty of fatherhood
Not too far away

At the funeral of an aunt I asked him
Why he came back he said
I never left I was always here
What are you talking about

I could tell from his eyes he was right
I had imagined everything

My father's pride Mother's tears
A sister's illness red-brown blood
Filling the hearth

Even the joy short-lived
of his occasional returns

& the silence when he left
that can never be written down

ACKNOWLEDGEMENTS

This book has taken slightly longer than I anticipated. It's true to say it owes everything to the intervention of some pretty special people. Thanks go first to Aaron & the team at Broken Sleep for seeing the light in these poems & for investing in them as a collection. I would also like to acknowledge:

Jack Caradoc at Dreich Press, for the first show of faith.

David Kinloch, without whom.
Liam & Owen, the real stars.
Kate, my light.

LAY OUT YOUR UNREST